# WILDLIFE OF SOUTH AFRICA

INTRODUCTION   On the sundrenched savannahs of Africa, a kingdom exists in perfect harmony with Nature. Where natural laws govern the survival of each species; where Nature takes care of her own in a circle of life as old as time itself, there is a balance, a serenity which man can only observe with wonder.

Far from the desires which drive humanity, removed from any concept of greed or ambition, the animal kingdom remains united under a hierarchy which continues unchallenged, just as Nature decreed from the very beginning. The Big Five - lion, leopard, elephant, rhinoceros and buffalo, side by side with the smallest of antelope and the most humble of creatures in a vast bushveld landscape that is at the very heart of Africa.

SUPERIOR   Born to royalty, unquestionably the leader of this intricate animal realm, lion soon cast aside the playful nature of their youth to assume a regal demeanour in keeping with their title.

---

*Left and above: Undisputed leader of this domain*
*Opposite:  Cubs at play*

UNITED   Leader of the pack, he commands respect, defending his territory with legendary ferocity and a show of might. As his mate, she bears the responsibility of providing sustenance. Together, they live in harmony at the very pinnacle of the hierarchy which governs this wild territory.

---

*Heads bowed, a tranquil moment at the waterhole*

VIGILANT   She is born to provide.  A teacher, she passes on her skills to her young; a hunter, she pursues her prey with agility and focus. A female, she must wait until her mate has satisfied his hunger before she can assuage her own.

*Lioness, loving mother - ruthless hunter*

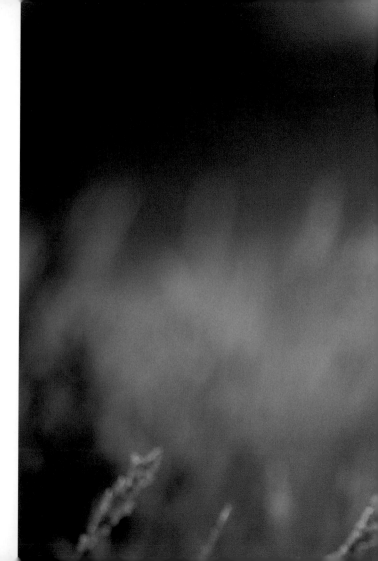

GRANDEUR   Colossal and imposing in their proportions, yet with a tender eye, and renowned for a loving heart.  Elephant exist in family groups; a mother will withstand any onslaught to protect a calf whether or not it is hers.  Bull elephant, statuesque by virtue of their sheer size, remain watchful and steadfastly protective of their herd.

_Dusty and weather-worn, to blend in with their environment_

TOGETHER   Like some pre-historic remnant of a bygone era, with withered skin and an encumbered gait, these great mammals lend a sense of dignity to an African bushveld scene, and inspire awe in all who are fortunate enough to view them.

*Right, and previous pages: Frolicking at the waterhole or trudging determinedly to a far-off destination, elephant are seldom alone*

CURIOUS    No storybook animal character can quite compare to this creature: absurdly tall, a petite head on an elongated neck, teetering along on stiletto legs which must be splayed to lower the head to take water. The giraffe is indeed a rather unique character in this African wildlife tapestry.

---

*Opposite: Tall enough to reach the tastiest shoots on the most distant of branches*
*Right: Long eyelashes and rounded horns give the giraffe a comical yet likeable countenance*

STEALTH  Few hunters are equipped with the speed, agility and precision of this predator, who will often gather every ounce of strength to drag a kill into the branches of a tree, where it may be relished without interruptions from hungry scavengers.

*Opposite and right: Prey has little chance of survival against the leopard, a steely-eyed hunter*

CAMOUFLAGED   Golden bushveld grasses envelop a dappled golden coat… a leopard, with every muscle taut, waits, cleverly hidden from Nature by Nature, for the perfect moment to pounce on unsuspecting prey.

---

*Left and opposite: Well concealed and well skilled, leopard are shy of human contact and sightings are rare*

INTENSE   Quite unaware of his noble attributes, a coat that inspires a fashion industry, and a head so often captured on canvas and cast in bronze - the leopard, another masterpiece wrought by the hand of the Creator.

SYMBIOSIS   A giant, hirsute buffalo is pecked free of parasites by the cheerful red billed oxpecker.  A tiny, skittish bird and a massive bulk of animal - one of Africa's Big Five - a curious illustration of Nature's laws at work.

CREATURES OF HABIT    A great cloud of dust…
a fearful vibration of the earth as hooves fly across the dry and
arid plain.  These creatures, with a generally placid disposition,
are at times ignited by the will to stampede, with great numbers
answering the call and moving en masse to unexplored territory.

*Wildebeest are characterised by a large head, wild shaggy mane and
sloping hindquarters*

SURVIVAL  A blur of black-and-white confuses the predator; zebra on the move are well adapted to outsmarting any attacker, as if deftly painted by a Master in the Arts, whose intricate brushstrokes serve as a tool for the creature's ultimate survival.

*Zebra mother and calf*

AGILE   A glimmer of colour through the tall grasses; a rush of action on the dusty veld.   The cheetah remains unrivalled for speed, like an arrow hurtling toward its target.

---

*Opposite: Juvenile cheetah siblings, soon to forsake the downy coat of their young years*
*Right: A deadly predator, the fastest land mammal*

THE LAW OF ABUNDANCE  A bushveld of such vast proportions, with a system cleverly devised by Nature to sustain its cheetah, leopard and lion predators. Indeed generous in her blessings, Nature clones great herds including impala, springbok and wildebeest for the occasional sacrifice, yet reserves many more to perpetuate the species and sustain this great Kingdom.

*Previous pages: Doting parent, loving mate - with razor sharp senses and a killer instinct*

*Opposite: Unmistakable markings of a ferocious feline*

NEIGHBOURS   The quiet golden pool at sunset.  First a ripple; then the waters part and a silver-skinned mass breaks the surface with a fine spray as the creature draws air.  From the banks, a sleepy onlooker rests as if cast in stone; then, in a rush of gnarled teeth, beady yellow eyes and whiplash tail, the crocodile joins his neighbour in the cool waters.

---

*Hippopotamus joust at the surface*

*Left: Ever-vigilant crocodile protects newly-hatched young*

*Opposite: A lythe swimmer and a deadly predator, both on land and in water*

TEMPERAMENTAL  Dinosaur-like in its contours; a horned beast well known for its split-second changes in temperament.  A squared lip distinguishes the white rhinoceros from the black.  Disturbed from its contented grazing, this enormous animal is capable of an instant change in direction and surprising speed and agility to intimidate the source of its anger.

*White rhinoceros family*

OBLIVIOUS     While the world evolves beyond these borders, battles are waged and history is made, this Kingdom continues in its own tradition of languid days and nights rested beneath a starlit sky.

---

*Previous pages: Rhinoceros enjoy a muddy bath and, like the elephant, are extremely loyal parents*
*Right: Black rhinoceros, identifiable by the hook of the lip*

SCAVENGERS   The lioness and her cubs relish the flesh of the kill: but they know they are not alone.   These scavengers pace at a distance, waiting impatiently for the pride to eat their fill, and for their turn to strip the carcass bare.

---

*Left: Hyena, renowned for their characteristic cackle and scavenging tactics*
*Above and opposite: Wild dog, alert and watchful for the remnants of the next kill*

PRIMATES   Endearingly affectionate… lively bright eyes glinting in the sunlight: primates have an eerie ability to mimic humans, particularly in expressing their emotions and in their grooming habits.

---

*Left: A vervet monkey, fiercely protective of her young*
*Right: These chacma baboon seem quite content to pose for a photograph*

ANTELOPE   Soulful dark eyes stare out at the world as if lost in thought; ears twitch constantly, fearful of a hidden predator. And at the first bleated warning, the herd leaps for shelter in a flurry of fur and flying hooves.

_Young impala - ever alert to danger_

AESTHETICS  Horns delicately curved, ornately spiralled, obtusely angled… accompanied by markings so intricate, so vivid - these creatures are a living tribute to the vision of Africa.

---

*Previous pages: Ringed horns and familiar markings of the springbok, so long revered as the symbol of the South African nation*
*Right: A herd of gemsbok*

EXOTIC   The animal kingdom is content to share its realm not only with mankind, but also with a variety of birdlife.   From the kaleidoscope colours of the lilac breasted roller to the deep petrol blue sheen of the glossy starling; the scavenging vulture to Nature's great show-bird, the ostrich - all are welcome to share this kingdom of wonder, existing in harmony, as Nature intended.

*Left: Hook-beaked vultures are seen wherever there is a fresh carcass*
*Right: The ostrich, flightless bird capable of fantastic running speeds*

PETITE   Where the lion walks proud and the leopard struts his noble presence, here too live creatures of a lesser stature; those whom Nature chose to compensate with visual appeal what they lack in size.

---

*Left: The hedgehog, with its very fashionable back of black-and-white quills*
*Page 60: Each scale perfectly positioned, the pangolin is a symmetrical marvel*
*Page 61: Cape fox mother and cub*

TEAMWORK   No man is an island… no animal stands alone.   Here in Africa's vast bushveld, each species looks after its own in an ecosystem orchestrated by Nature with unfaltering precision, unwaivering devotion.

---

*A family of suricate perch momentarily, enjoying the warm earth before scampering about the day's activities*

PHOTOGRAPHERS   Peter Chadwick - *pg 3a*  M Craig-Cooper - *pg 14*   Peter Craig-Cooper - *pg 49*   Nigel Dennis - *pg 1, 4b, 8, 12, 13,17, 20, 26, 28, 35, 36, 42, 43, 44, 46b, 52, 54, 57, 58, 60, 61, 62, 64, back cover*   Pat de la Harpe - *pgs 2a, 37, 38*   Roger de la Harpe - *pg 2b, 16, 22, 30, 39, 41, 46a, 50*   Martin Harvey - *cover, inside cover, pg 4a, 6, 10, 18, 31, 32, 47*   Lanz von Hörsten - *pg 33*   Richard du Toit - *pg 25, 48, 56*   James Wakelin - *pg 3b*   Jason Keywood - *pg 5, 19*   James Warwick - *pg 21*

Produced by Art Publishers (Pty) Ltd

*Durban, Johannesberg, Cape Town*